WHISPERED VISIONS OF THE SOUL (PART 2)

PRAGNA

Made with ♥ on the Notion Press Platform
www.notionpress.com

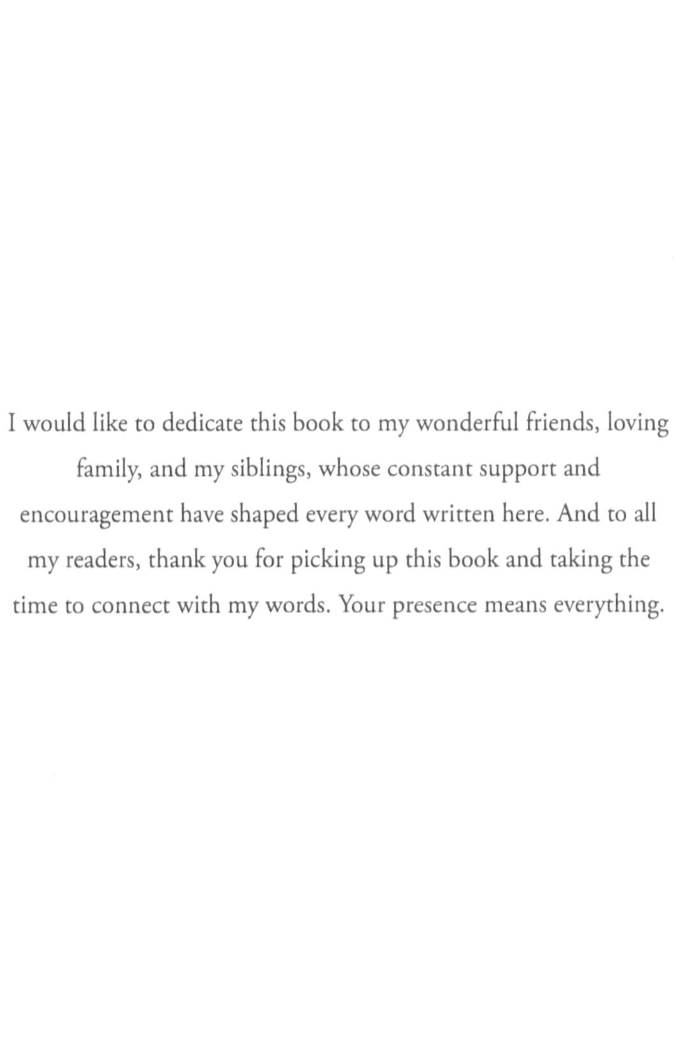

I would like to dedicate this book to my wonderful friends, loving family, and my siblings, whose constant support and encouragement have shaped every word written here. And to all my readers, thank you for picking up this book and taking the time to connect with my words. Your presence means everything.

Contents

Contents

Foreword

Words have the power to heal, to hold, and to help us rediscover the light we once thought was lost. Whispered Visions of the Soul – Part 2 is not just a book—it's a reflection of emotions, quietly born beneath the clouds, in moments of silence. Poetry, when written from the heart, can echo louder than any voice in the world.

In this collection, I've poured fragments of growth, the ache of letting go, the joy found in small things, and the journey of falling in love with oneself again. These pages are pieces of my soul—but I hope you find pieces of yours too.

Thank you for holding my words close. May they whisper to your heart exactly when you need them most.

Preface

Whispered Visions of the Soul Part 2 is a journey that began with stillness and soul-searching. This book is not just about poetry, it's about moments.

The quiet ones, the heavy ones, and the ones that make us feel alive again.

Each piece in this collection came from a place of honesty written in solitude, inspired by fleeting thoughts, memories, emotions, and the little shifts that shape who we become. It speaks of new beginnings, silent strength, the ache of change, and the beauty of learning to embrace yourself all over again.

This book is a reminder that healing isn't loud it's gentle. And even in our quietest moments, there's a story waiting to be heard.

Acknowledgements

This book would not have been possible without the love and encouragement of those who stood beside me when I had no words to share.

To my family, thank you for believing in me, for your endless support, and for encouraging me to dream, even in silence. You've held space for both my quiet and my growth, and for that, I'm forever grateful.

To every soul who reads this book and finds even a flicker of light your presence gives purpose to my words.
May you discover your own whispered truths in these pages... the kind that gently guide you back to yourself.

A heartfelt thank you to Ridhi, the talented illustrator, whose art so beautifully echoes the soul of these words. Your vision brought emotion and depth to life, and I'm so grateful for your creative spirit.

1. Somewhere

That smile gone somewhere,
That bright love gone somewhere.
Empty house, locked door,
Once filled with joy, now keyed in the drawer.
That first shiny eyes in the morning and the last bright smile,
That smile gone somewhere,
That bright love gone somewhere.
Moon mocked my loneliness,
That sun now sleeps in empty air.
That smile gone somewhere,
That bright love gone somewhere.

2. Sparkling Eyes

• 2 •

Now, you are in the stars, between the clouds and the moon.
Looking up reminds me of you,
That smiling face and those sparkling eyes.
Hugging you is a memory that lingers in my mind and heart,
A warmth I still can't forget.
But now, you are in the stars, between the clouds and the moon.

3. Old Bonds

Old bonds died when the time came,

To leave the ones who loved them with no shame.

New bonds took them to a new place,

A new beginning with a better pace.

Still, the ones who stayed like the old are in the same state,

Same pace, but now on a better stage.

While the new ones face their issues to this date,

Still exploring unfamiliar gates.

As they said, those who love and cherish you will never change,

But the ones who came as a lesson will face the same pain and rage,

Old bonds died when the time came,

To leave the ones who loved them with no shame....

4. Puzzly Puzzle

My life became a puzzling puzzle,
Each piece got hidden in life's muzzle.
Where every step feels like a warning buzzer,
And every move plays out like a blockbuster.
Faces around me wear a mask,
Each hiding behind their own task.
Yes, my life became a puzzling puzzle,
Each piece got hidden in life's muzzle.
They say this year wasn't the best,
But I've learned to worry less about the rest.
The pain and hurt I quietly bear,
Only made me strong, more self-aware.
My life became a puzzling puzzle,
Each piece got hidden in life's muzzle.
Sometimes I just want to be that little girl,
Handled with care, like a soft curl.
Craving a shoulder where I can lean,
To share my worries, like when I was a teen.
But still my life remains a puzzling puzzle,
Each piece got hidden in life's muzzle.

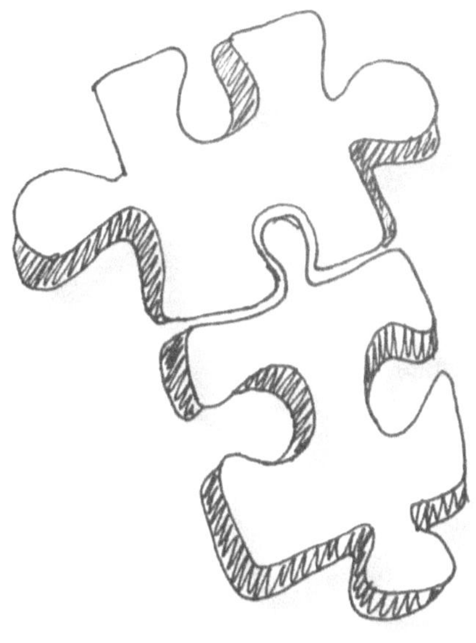

5. Phase

When everyone was running in their own races,
You were stuck in the same phase with the old faces.
You found yourself caught in the same old spot,
As if that was everything you ever got.
Hurt and betrayal were the lessons you learned,
Your heart felt scorched, like it had burned.
You can't think straight,
You can't make a face,
Numbing your nerves,
Your eyes only observe.
You can neither leave nor stay,
All you have left is to pray.
Grateful for someone by your side,
A quiet place where you can hide.
Watching the clouds move in one direction,
You slowly begin to build a better connection.
Yet still, you're stuck in the same old phase,
With the same old thoughts and familiar faces.

6. New me

I found the new me,
The better me,
The one who wants to do her best,
The one who longs for peaceful rest.
The cloudy sky with no storms,
Discovering herself in different forms.
I found the new me,
The better me,
The one who knows the way,
The one who knows how to stay.
Breaking the boundaries that she once feared,
Building a world where everything is crystal clear.
I found the new me,
The better me,
The one who makes herself a priority,
The one who walks with quiet maturity.
Handling things like a pro,
But still has to learn many things to grow.
I found the new me,
The better me,
The one who loves to dress,
The one who won't be a second guess.
Painting the soul with different colors,

Hiding the pain in different covers.
I found the new me,
The better me,
The one who wants nothing to lose or gain,
The one who doesn't want to feel any pain.
Admiring the rain as a beauty,
Still shows up as if it was her duty.
Finally, I found the new
And better me.

7. Dreams

The list of dreams that I wish to come true,
A painted flower in the color blue,
That dress with silver crystals,
In the world of blazing pistols.
The list of dreams that I wish to come true,
A painted flower in the color blue,
Wearing high heels with a shiny stone,
Showing you are all grown,
But still want to be the one with a crown,
With the sparkling eyes filled with the color brown.
The list of dreams that I wish to come true,
A painted flower in the color blue,
Dazzling lights with a way filled with daisies,
Still get excited after seeing someone with the cute babies.
Wishing everything is a dream,
Where me and you will be the bestest team.

8. Covered

The more I wash my hands,

The more they got covered with the sand,

The sand of guilt,

The guilt of some words that can't be turned to quilt,

The more I wash my hands,

The more they got covered in bands,

The bands that tie me,

The strings of getting hurt that can't set me free,

The more I wash my hands,

The more they got covered with dirt that expands,

The dirt of betrayal,

That betrayal that made me stand in a trial,

The more I wash my hands,

The more they got covered in mud that commands,

The mud that commands the silence,

The silence that zipped my words and suffocate my presence,

The more I wash my hands,

The more they got covered in...

9. Lie

That was a lie
When you had reasons to speak badly,
When you were giving off vibes madly,
That was a lie.
The time we spent together,
The mirror that reflected us as one, better.
That was a lie.
The truth that was covered and,
Our bond started from a lie, and then...
It changed me while picking the broken pieces of us,
That graced all the things, thus,
It was all a lie,
From the start to the end happened to be a sweet goodbye...

10. Tatooed Signs

Roaming around here and there,
You were sending me a message to bear.
Your flip is a fine sign,
Like connecting me to angels it feels divine.
Those two years were the best,
I truly trusted you that day with the rest.
Tattooed you on my arm,
To help me think positively and keep me calm.
Showing that you will grow and change,
And I am growing, beyond several range.
Sitting in the corner in the dark,
Panic attacks and tears a lifelong mark.
Seeing you somewhere on a flower feels like a dream,
Flying across with a beautiful color cream.
Thank you for giving me a sign,
I'll make it last and turn it into something fine.

11. Painted Skies

Like a painted story,
Like a beautiful glory,
God painted you and me,
Always together and set to be free.
Sky with a tint,
My love for you is a hint.
Like two swans together,
Always there for each other.
Like a painted story,
Like a glamorous glory,
Just like the white moon and the yellow sun,
Our love for each other always burns.
The care for each other
Remains till together forever.
Like a painted story,
Like a glamorous glory,
How those chocolaty eyes look only for me,
The comfort is just like waves in the shining sea.
The air I breathe
Is just like me sitting beneath,
Under a tree that exhales the peace.
Like a painted story,
Like a beautiful glory.

• 14 •

12. Book of Silver

It's always the book of silver,
that makes the life full of glitter.
Still remember the first time,
when a book taught me big life limes.
When those lime met with a beat—
is it sour or is it sweet?
It's always the book of silver,
that makes the life full of glitter.
Wanted the day sprouts form the night,
where books are my bright sunlight.
And wanted that day diluted into night,
where books were the last friends in the last holy light.
It's always the book of silver,
that makes the life full of glitter.
When I lay I wanted to say,
I always laugh and cry with you,
because you changed my whole world,
just like Cinderella's glass shoe.
Started from "Once upon a time,"
now seems like a crime,
where we are the culprits,
and the books have to pick just a bit.

It's always the books of silver,

that makes the life full of glitter.

Just like a butterfly,

they taught me how to fly high up the sky.

From twinkle twinkle little stars,

to hiding those scary scars,

books were always there,

while I was grasping for air.

Books are my bulletproof shield,

that make me fully healed.

In a battle of deadly deed,

it's always the books of silver,

that makes the life full of glitter.

When grandma with her book sat on her armchair with her

spectacles on—

now that time has really gone.

Those books of hers are like the prosperity of family,

where we cherish those monuments lovingly.

Books are the chief part of our life,

that keeps us alive.

Because it's always the book of silver,

that makes the life full of glitter,

that makes the life full of glitter...

13. Rainfall

Falling of every drop of rain
brings pain to my heart.
The time we spent together
became a beautiful memory.
Tears are whelming in my eyes
while spending the time remembering you.
Time passes and made me stronger,
but I hope to be happy with every next rain.
Life is going smooth,
but not the way I wanted it to.
The dreams are coming through,
but everything is shattering
since you have gone too far from me.

14. Becoming Her Again

I am becoming her again,
The old me once again,
The one that adjusts with everyone,
The one that trusts no one,
The one that loves nature,
The one that loves to nurture.

As I am becoming her again,
The old me once again,
The one that smiles without any grade,
The one who doesn't care who's on the parade,
The one that builds her esteem,
The one that builds her own team.

I am becoming her again,
The old me once again.

15. A Memory

The day that I still can't believe was true,
The memory of you still sometimes lingers in my head,
Still remember the day when the sky turned red.
Having so much fun together,
When you became a child with me,
Hop on the scooter with a black bucket hat with you,
Loved being honest and true with you.
Holding your hands as a child is a precious memory,
Swinging on a swing with you is like a painted scenery.
The puzzle you gave me is still with me,
Wrapping it in a paper gracefully, always love to see.
Still there, waiting for you like a little girl,
Love to hear the name calling "Pannu" from downstairs.
Now the home feels empty without you,
Hope you see me from above behind the clouds, watching too.

16. The Weight of Almost

The heaviness of almost there,
when finally everything was settling here,
The rage between you and me started to disappear,
The time started when everything is getting cleared,
The heaviness of almost there,
when finally everything was settling there.

17. The Two Sided Story

When you hear the two-sided story,
You will know the actual glory.
One side only gives misunderstanding,
Presenting the one as too demanding.
When you hear the two-sided story,
You will know the actual glory.
The love and patience start to vanish,
Making the relationship too lavish.
Ego builds the wall of a house,
Then one becomes like an abandoned room in a house.
When you hear the two-sided story,
You will know the actual glory.
Feeling the pain,
Having nothing to gain.
Now the tie,
Forever gone, just in the white sky.
When you hear the two-sided story,
You will know the actual glory...

18. Too Far

Through the window of heart,
Still too far from the new start,
The calmness of wind,
The light of the sun pinned,
The tree standing alone,
Maybe all the plan was known,
The story was at fault from the start,
Maybe that represents the weakening of the heart,

Through the window of heart,
Still too far from the new start,
The waves in the ocean are the proof,
I was standing alone still on the roof.
Through the window of heart,
Still too far from the new start.

19. Letting Go

Letting go gracefully,
Finally letting go faithfully.
The talks, the chats,
Still can't forget the way that was.
The small giggles
Still now tickle.
The hoping together
Is gone forever.
Because I am letting go gracefully,
Finally letting go faithfully.
Not bounding you to talk with me,
Still want you to remember the original me.
The drama was there from the start,
All the hurt was stored in a small cart.
But I am letting go gracefully,
Letting go, all very faithfully.

20. Till the day

Till the day I die,
Till the day I die,
I want to feel the happiness carried by the wind,
To be embraced by the love of blooming flowers,
Standing before a tower, tall and proud,
I want to feel the chill of the ocean waves,
As they whisper secrets to the shore.
Till the day I die,
I want to soak in the warmth of the rising sun,
To rest in the calmness of drifting clouds,
To lose myself in the glow of the midnight stars,
Till the day I die.
Till the day I die...

21. Smiling Eyes

Holding hands with smiling eyes,

We are bound with forever ties.

When the eyes talk,

And the steps we walk,

The path that we long,

Is what makes us strong.

Slowly and steadily, we keep moving,

Stepping on one stair at a time and improving.

Holding hands with smiling eyes,

We are bound with forever ties.

Making the castles,

Shaping them with chisels,

Wearing a bracelet of silver,

Sitting down near the river.

Holding hands with smiling eyes,

We are bound with forever ties.

22. Closed Eyes

Dots on the wall,
Waiting for the final call.
Till the eyes get closed,
Want to remember the place where the poetry composed.
Building the home with bricks,
Trying every new trick.
Talking with a calm face,
Want to escape from the life race.
Want to be free with no chains,
That give the unlimited pains.
Still waiting for the final call,
Till the eyes get closed.

23. Own Choice

Tied with a silver wire of depression,
Overthinking became an expression.
Red blood flowing down my hands,
With half-tied hair strands.

Eyes filled with tears,
Getting erased by the dark that everyone fears.
It's beautiful to see everything becoming accurate,
Like in a deep sea you alone navigate.

Running from the sweetness,
As it became my biggest weakness.
Shouting with no voice,
Everything was my own choice.

Standing on the top of a building,
With no one shielding.

Tied with a silver wire of depression,
Overthinking became an expression.
Standing with trembling legs,
Where the eyes beg.
With a knife on my throat,

Getting the lessons life taught.
Standing with cold feet,
Where only the heart beats.

A drop of water,
Finding a better potter.
Tied with a silver wire of depression,
Overthinking became an expression.

24. You

I found your gentle voice,
In this delightful silence, I made my choice.
You are the one,
Being together is always fun.
Your smile brightens my sky,
I thought it was time to give love a try.
Wrapping my hand around your arm,
I finally found our charm.
Sitting on grass in a flowery gown,
Living our days in a pretty town.
Sleeping with the moon, waking with the sun,
Side by side on a joyful run.
I found your gentle voice,
In this delightful silence, I made my choice.
Me doing the laundry,
You setting the boundary.
Picking out a sweet bun,
Together having endless fun.
Smiling softly from the heart,
You feel like a work of art.
I found your gentle voice,
In this delightful silence, I made my choice,
My choice was choosing you.

25. Moonlight

Moonlight on the broken glass,
Watching while sitting on damp grass.
Light reflects upon the mirror,
Skin getting even more fairer.
Sitting down in a black dress,
Warned her before not to be obsessed.
Seeking love can dim your light,
Then you want to hold the memories tight.
Moonlight on the broken glass,
Watching while sitting on damp grass.
Lips colored with the shade of blue,
Hair now wet it hardly looks true.
Swollen ankles, straps of heels on it,
Still trying hard to firmly stand on it.
Moonlight on the broken glass,
Watching while sitting on damp grass.
Remember your smiling face,
Now I just have your only trace.
A bracelet resting in my hand,
Wishing for a stable land.
The river flowing down the shore,
You became my lovable memory and my only hope.

26. Healing after Goodbye

Healing after a goodbye,
Now makes me want to give it a try.
The sensation of self-love,
Makes me want to rise above.
God has reasons for everything,
Maybe replacing a good thing with a better something.
We all met by plans,
That can't be handled with just our hands.
Love, hate, friendships the relations we describe,
Yet sometimes, they're the hardest things to find.
Life is a circle of lessons,
Some bring hurt, and some come as blessings.
'Cause I want to give it a try,
The healing after a goodbye...

27. The Peaceful Life

Winds gushed through my face,
Leaving peace as a trace.
Birds chirping above my head,
Waiting for sweet morning bread.

The old tree in front,
Where a parrot sits, making a stunt.
I am too happy to see the view,
My heart felt light, my soul anew.

Clouds painted in the sky,
Polished with a nice try.
Sitting on a bench,
Wanting to be a dreamer lost in nature's hue.

28. Mirror

Some admire,
Some are tired,
Some feel sleepy,
Some a little creepy.
Some are beautiful,
Some are youthful,
Some speak the truth,
Some are just seeing their tooth.
Some wear a mask of happiness,
Some show gratefulness,
Some are a little cranky,
Not all are that frank, see?
But all are there in the front,
While being blunt.
You play the role of reflection,
Not judging anyone's tension.
Happy to call you a mirror,
Making everything feel set and clearer.

From The Author

As I bring this collection of emotions, verses, and memories to a close, I want to thank every soul who paused for a moment to read my words and feel them deeply. These poems are not just written pieces they are fragments of my heart stitched together with pain, healing, love, and growth.

Each line has been born from a moment lived a tear, a smile, a heartbreak, a whisper of hope. If my words found a place in your heart, made you feel seen, comforted, or understood, then I have done what I came here to do.

To anyone still trying to find themselves, battling silent wars, or carrying memories that weigh heavy. I hope this book feels like a hand reaching out to you. Because you are not alone.

This is not the end, it's a beginning. A reminder that even in the darkest hours, you are growing, becoming, and healing. Slowly, quietly, beautifully.

With love,

Pragna

www.ingramcontent.com/pod-product-compliance
Lightning Source LLC
Chambersburg PA
CBHW031245130726
47988CB00008B/3252